HOLT McDOUGAL LITERATURE

Online Edition
Selection Supplement
Grade 7

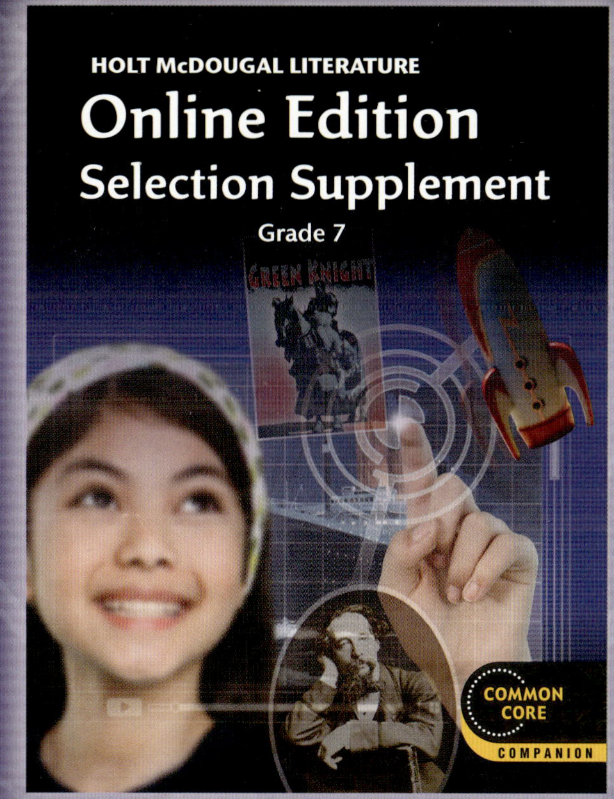

HOLT McDOUGAL

 HOUGHTON MIFFLIN HARCOURT

ART CREDITS

COVER, TITLE PAGE
top left © Kit Houghton/Corbis; *top right* © Randy Faris/Corbis;
bottom center The Granger Collection, New York;
background The Titanic, Gordon Johnson. Oil on paper. © Margaret Johnson/SuperStock

ISBN 13: 978-0-547-65018-0

3 4 5 6 7 8 9 10 1420 20 19 18 17 16 15 14 13 12 11

4500308768   A B C D E F G

TABLE OF CONTENTS

Plot, Setting, and Character

What makes you willing to spend two hours at the movie theater or a week reading a book? Is it the thrill of action-packed events or a connection to the characters? Is it a fascination with the setting, such as a faraway galaxy? Plot, conflict, setting, and characters all play a role in holding your interest in a story.

COMMON CORE

Included in this workshop:
RL 1 Cite several pieces of textual evidence to support analysis of what the text says explicitly. **RL 3** Analyze how different elements of a story interact.

Part 1: What Drives a Story?

The idea for a story might begin with an observation or a thought that interests a writer. To build a story from that idea, a writer creates a plot structure using the elements of fiction listed here.

- **Setting** is the time and place of the action. The time might be the historical era, the season, or the time of day. The place might be a country, a neighborhood, or a room. In many stories, setting influences the plot and affects the characters' feelings.

- **Characters** are the people, animals, or imaginary creatures that take part in a story. The characters' behavior affects what happens.

- **Plot** is the series of events in a story. The plot usually centers on a **conflict,** a struggle between different forces. Conflict fuels the action, moving the plot forward. A conflict can be external or internal.

TYPE OF CONFLICT	EXAMPLE
 **External Conflict** is a struggle between a character and an outside force. This force might be another character, a group of characters, or nature.	A sea captain attempts to guide his boat to shore in the middle of a deadly storm. ▶ **(sea captain vs. nature)** *Other Examples* • A boxer faces an opponent. • A girl has a fight with friends.
 **Internal Conflict** is a struggle within a character's mind. This kind of conflict happens when a character must deal with opposing thoughts or feelings.	A girl strongly disagrees with her friends, but she wants them to like her. Should she speak her mind or stay silent? ▶ **(girl vs. herself)** *Other Examples* • Admit needing help or do it alone? • Take a risk or play it safe?

This author draws you into the story by providing specific details about the setting. How might the setting influence what happens?

from # The Clay Marble

Novel by **Minfong Ho**

The last rays of afternoon sun were filtering through the forest as we approached the Border. Gradually the trees thinned out and the path widened. Several trails merged into ours. It seemed as if all the paths out of Cambodia were converging on this one spot on the Thai border.

5   I could barely contain my excitement. I imagined mountains of rice lining the horizon, and piles of tools and fishnets everywhere. Perhaps there would even be mounds of sweet moist coconut cakes and banana fritters. "Hurry," I urged my brother.

    Yet, as we finally emerged from the forest, all we could see was a vast

10 barren plain dotted with shrubs and scraggly trees, flat and desolate.

Close Read

1. What details about the setting do you find in lines 1–4? One detail has been boxed.

2. Describe what the narrator expects to see when she crosses the border. Then describe what she actually sees. How might the actual setting affect the narrator and the story?

Here, a girl watches from the deck of a ship as her brother is left on a deserted island. What do you learn about the conflict in this excerpt?

from # Island of the Blue Dolphins

Novel by **Scott O'Dell**

Against my will, I screamed.

Chief Matasaip grasped my arm.

"We cannot wait for Ramo," he said. "If we do, the ship will be driven on the rocks."

5   "We must!" I shouted. "We must!"

    "The ship will come back for him on another day," Matasaip said. "He will be safe. There is food for him to eat and water to drink and places to sleep."

    "No," I cried.

10   Matasaip's face was like stone. He was not listening.

Close Read

1. Describe the conflict the girl experiences.

2. Is the girl's conflict internal or external? Explain how you know.

Part 2: Plot Development

No matter who the characters are, where the action takes place, or what conflicts occur, a story has a plot. Usually, a story begins by introducing a main character who has a conflict. The story then develops around this conflict. Important events move the story forward, often explaining past or present actions, and **foreshadowing,** or hinting at, future actions. As the story moves on, the character must find a solution to the conflict. Once the problem is solved, the story ends. This process is known as **plot development.**

A typical plot has five stages of action. By understanding these stages, you will know what to look for in a story as you follow it closely. For example, at the beginning—or **exposition**—of a story, pay attention to the details that tell you about the characters, the setting, and any potential conflicts.

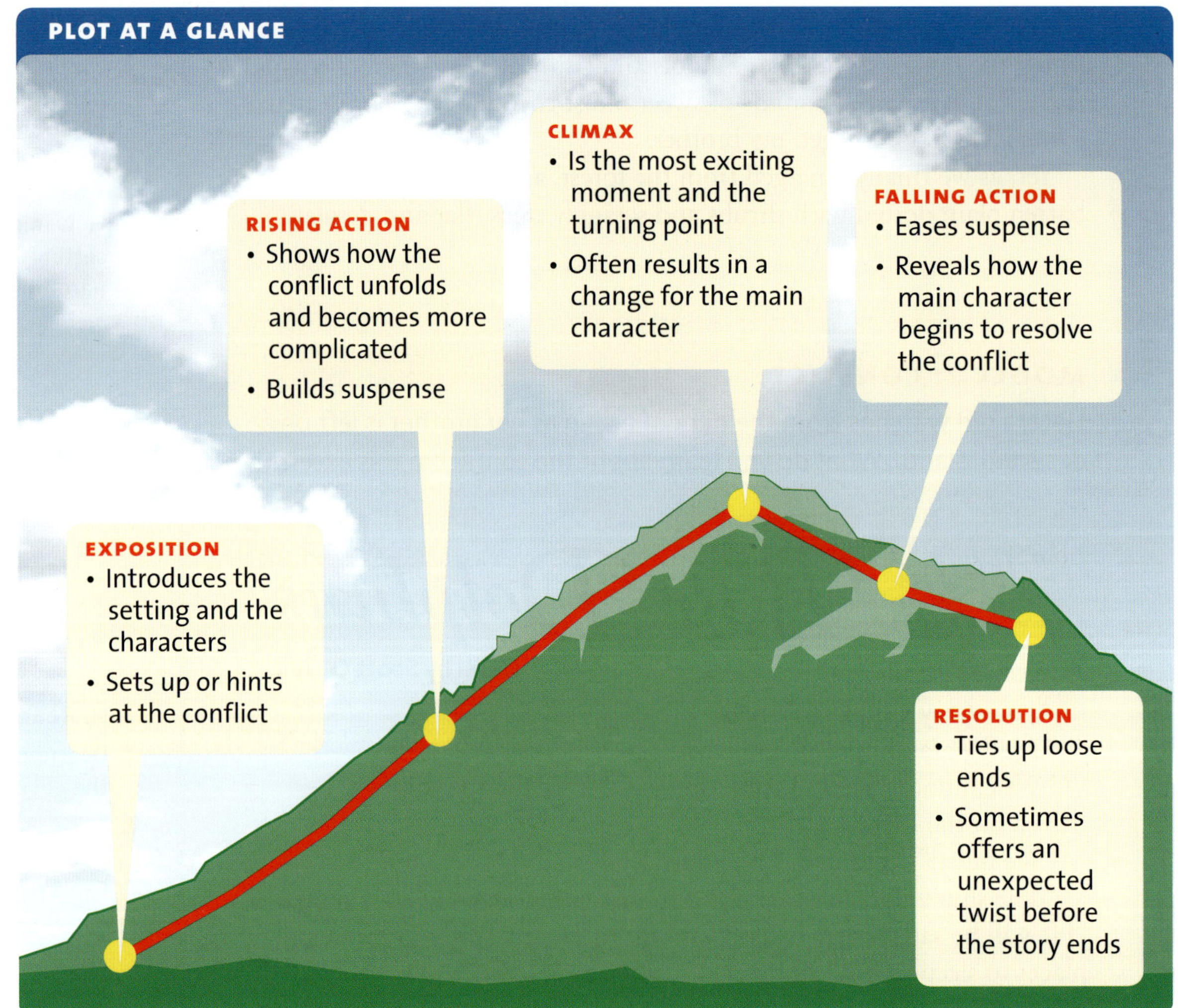

MODEL 1: EXPOSITION

What do you learn about the setting and the conflict in the exposition of this story?

from
Last Cover

Short story by **Paul Annixter**

I'm not sure I can tell you what you want to know about my brother; but everything about the pet fox is important, so I'll tell all that from the beginning.

It goes back to a winter afternoon after I'd hunted the woods all
5   day for a sign of our lost pet. I remember the way my mother looked up as I came into the kitchen. Without my speaking, she knew what had happened. For six hours I had walked, reading signs, looking for a delicate print in the damp soil or even a hair that might have told of a red fox passing that way—but I had found nothing.

Close Read

1. What can you tell about the setting in which the main character lives? Find specific details that describe the setting.

2. Review the boxed details. Describe the conflict that the main character faces. What does this conflict suggest the story will be about?

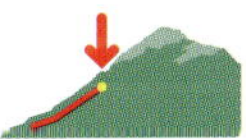

MODEL 2: RISING ACTION

At the beginning of this story, lonely Mr. Peters is granted three wishes. He uses his first wish to ask for a wife. In the rising action, what do you learn about the conflict that results from this wish?

from
THE THIRD WISH

Short story by **Joan Aiken**

One evening he was returning home along the river path when he saw Leita in front of him, down by the water. A swan had sailed up to the verge and she had her arms round its neck and the swan's head rested against her cheek. She was weeping, and as he came nearer he
5   saw that tears were rolling, too, from the swan's eyes.

"Leita, what is it?" he asked, very troubled.

"This is my sister," she answered. "I can't bear being separated from her."

Now he understood that Leita was really a swan from the forest, and
10 this made him very sad because when a human being marries a bird it always leads to sorrow.

Close Read

1. Reread the boxed text. What conflict is Mr. Peters facing?

2. During the rising action, the plot moves toward the climax. What future decision or action might this situation hint at, or foreshadow?

Part 3: Analyze the Text

In this story, an elegant dinner party turns dangerous when an uninvited "guest" makes an appearance. As you read, use what you've just learned about plot, conflict, and setting to analyze the story.

The Dinner Party

Short story by
Mona Gardner

The country is India. A large dinner party is being given in an up-country station by a colonial official[1] and his wife. The guests are army officers and government attachés[2] and their wives, and an American naturalist.[3]

5 At one side of the long table a spirited discussion springs up between a young girl and a colonel. The girl insists women have long outgrown the jumping-on-a-chair-at-the-sight-of-a-mouse era, that they are not as fluttery as their grandmothers. The colonel says they are, explaining that women haven't the actual nerve control of men. The other men at
10 the table agree with him.

"A woman's unfailing reaction in any crisis," the colonel says, "is to scream. And while a man may feel like it, yet he has that ounce more of control than a woman has. And that last ounce is what counts!"

The American scientist does not join in the argument, but sits
15 watching the faces of the other guests. As he looks, he sees a strange expression come over the face of the hostess. She is staring straight ahead, the muscles of her face contracting slightly. With a small gesture she summons the native boy standing behind her chair. She whispers to him. The boy's eyes widen: he turns quickly and leaves the room.

---

1. **colonial official:** a person holding a position in the British government ruling India.

2. **attachés** (ăt′ə-shāz′)**:** people who assist an ambassador.

3. **naturalist:** a person who studies living things by observing them directly.

1. What do you learn about the setting in the exposition?

2. Explain what the young girl and the colonel are arguing about in lines 5–13. What might this topic foreshadow?

3. Find two details in lines 14–19 that might foreshadow future events in the story. One detail has been boxed.

20 No one else sees this, nor the boy when he puts a bowl of milk on the verandah[4] outside the glass doors.

The American comes to with a start. In India, milk in a bowl means only one thing. It is bait for a snake. He realizes there is a cobra in the room.

25 He looks up at the rafters[5]—the likeliest place—and sees they are bare. Three corners of the room, which he can see by shifting only slightly, are empty. In the fourth corner a group of servants stand, waiting until the next course can be served. The American realizes there is only one place left—under the table.

30 His first impulse is to jump back and warn the others. But he knows the commotion will frighten the cobra and it will strike. He speaks quickly, the quality of his voice so arresting that it sobers everyone.

"I want to know just what control everyone at this table has. I will count three hundred—that's five minutes—and not one of you is to 35 move a single muscle. The persons who move will forfeit 50 rupees.[6] Now! Ready!"

The 20 people sit like stone images while he counts. He is saying ". . . two hundred and eighty . . ." when, out of the corner of his eye, he sees the cobra emerge and make for the bowl of milk. Four or five 40 screams ring out as he jumps to slam shut the verandah doors.

"You certainly were right, Colonel!" the host says. "A man has just shown us an example of real control."

"Just a minute," the American says, turning to his hostess, "there's one thing I'd like to know. Mrs. Wynnes, how did you know that cobra was 45 in the room?"

A faint smile lights up the woman's face as she replies. "Because it was lying across my foot."

---

4. **verandah:** a long porch, usually roofed, along the side of a building.

5. **rafters:** wooden beams that support a roof.

6. **rupees** (ro͞o-pēz′): Indian units of money.

---

4. Reread lines 22–24. What is the main conflict? Explain whether it is internal or external.

Close Read
Climax (Lines 37–40)

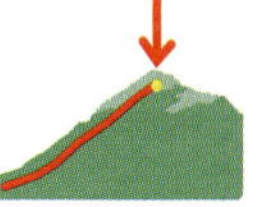

5. What happens at the climax, or the most exciting moment?

Close Read
Falling Action and Resolution (Lines 41–47)

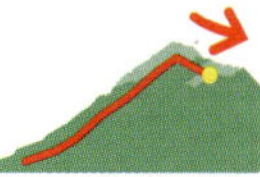

6. At what point in the falling action does the tension begin to ease? Explain.

7. What surprise is revealed in the resolution? How does this explain Mrs. Wynnes's earlier reaction?

Dark They Were, and Golden-Eyed

Science Fiction by Ray Bradbury

HISTORY Video link at **thinkcentral.com**

VIDEO TRAILER THiNK central   KEYWORD: HML7-460

Can where you are CHANGE who you are?

Your hobbies, interests, and habits often depend on the climate you are used to and the people and places you encounter every day. If you were to move away from everything you know, how much of who you are would change, and how much would stay the same? In "Dark They Were, and Golden-Eyed," a family moves to a very different environment and gets the chance to find out.

DISCUSS With a group, discuss your thoughts about the question at the top of the page. Take turns answering the question and explaining your reasons. Record the group's responses on a chart like the one shown.

Can Where You Are Change Who You Are?		
Name	Yes or No	Why or Why Not?

TEXT ANALYSIS: MOOD

Has a story ever made you feel hopeful, nervous, or completely terrified? The feeling you get from a story is called the **mood.** Writers create a mood by

- carefully choosing words to describe the **plot, setting,** and **characters**
- showing what characters think and how they talk

Identifying mood can help you understand a story. As you read "Dark They Were, and Golden-Eyed," think about how it makes you feel, and what words affect you.

READING STRATEGY: READING SCIENCE FICTION

In **science fiction,** writers often explore the future. They blend scientific facts and theories and familiar elements of real life with their own ideas.

Although science fiction writers portray future times and places, their themes often comment on the problems of today's world. As you read Ray Bradbury's story, use a chart to note characteristics of science fiction.

Characteristics of Science Fiction	Examples in the Story
scientific information	
familiar elements of life today	
imaginary worlds and situations	

Review: **Make Inferences**

▲ VOCABULARY IN CONTEXT

Bradbury's **word choice** affects the **mood** of his story. Match each numbered word or phrase with a vocabulary word.

WORD LIST			
	convivial	forlorn	recede
	dwindle	muse	subtly
	flimsy	pendulum	

1. friendly
2. indirectly
3. hanging weight
4. decrease
5. become distant
6. daydream
7. lonely
8. breakable

Complete the activities in your **Reader/Writer Notebook.**

Ray Bradbury
born 1920

An Early Start
Ray Bradbury credits his mother for encouraging his imagination. She loved films and started taking her son to see them when he was only 3. By age 8, Bradbury had developed a love for both science fiction and the planet Mars. Bradbury wrote his first Martian stories when he was 12. Just before his 21st birthday, Bradbury sold his first story. That began a career filled with bestsellers, awards, and a lasting love of writing.

Man with a Mission Bradbury believes that one purpose of science fiction is to warn about negative things that might happen in the future if care is not taken in the present. Some of his writing reflects his worries about where our society is headed.

BACKGROUND TO THE STORY

Red Planet Mars has been the setting of many science fiction films and stories, including "Dark They Were, and Golden-Eyed." Films and stories about Mars rarely give a realistic description of the planet, but they often incorporate elements of actual scientific research and developments in space travel.

461

DARK THEY WERE, AND GOLDEN-EYED

RAY BRADBURY

The rocket metal cooled in the meadow winds. Its lid gave a bulging *pop.* From its clock interior stepped a man, a woman, and three children. The other passengers whispered away across the Martian meadow, leaving the man alone among his family.

The man felt his hair flutter and the tissues of his body draw tight as if he were standing at the center of a vacuum. His wife, before him, seemed almost to whirl away in smoke. The children, small seeds, might at any instant be sown to all the Martian climes.

The children looked up at him, as people look to the sun to tell
10 what time of their life it is. His face was cold.

"What's wrong?" asked his wife.

"Let's get back on the rocket." Ⓐ

"Go back to Earth?"

"Yes! Listen!"

The wind blew as if to flake away their identities. At any moment the Martian air might draw his soul from him, as marrow comes from a white bone. He felt submerged in a chemical that could dissolve his intellect and burn away his past.

They looked at Martian hills that time had worn with a crushing
20 pressure of years. They saw the old cities, lost in their meadows, lying like children's delicate bones among the blowing lakes of grass.

"Chin up, Harry," said his wife. "It's too late. We've come over sixty million miles."

The children with their yellow hair hollered at the deep dome of Martian sky. There was no answer but the racing hiss of wind through the stiff grass. **B**

He picked up the luggage in his cold hands. "Here we go," he said— a man standing on the edge of a sea, ready to wade in and be drowned.

They walked into town.

30 Their name was Bittering. Harry and his wife Cora; Dan, Laura, and David. They built a small white cottage and ate good breakfasts there, but the fear was never gone. It lay with Mr. Bittering and Mrs. Bittering, a third unbidden partner at every midnight talk, at every dawn awakening.

"I feel like a salt crystal," he said, "in a mountain stream, being washed away. We don't belong here. We're Earth people. This is Mars. It was meant for Martians. For heaven's sake, Cora, let's buy tickets for home!"

But she only shook her head. "One day the atom bomb will fix Earth. Then we'll be safe here."

"Safe and insane!"

40 *Tick-tock, seven o'clock* sang the voice-clock; *time to get up.* And they did.
Something made him check everything each morning—warm hearth, potted blood-geraniums—precisely as if he expected something to be amiss. The morning paper was toast-warm from the 6 A.M. Earth rocket. He broke its seal and tilted it at his breakfast place. He forced himself to be **convivial**. **C**

"Colonial days all over again," he declared. "Why, in ten years there'll be a million Earthmen on Mars. Big cities, everything! They said we'd fail. Said the Martians would resent our invasion. But did we find any Martians? Not a living soul! Oh, we found their empty cities, but no one
50 in them. Right?"

A river of wind submerged the house. When the windows ceased rattling Mr. Bittering swallowed and looked at the children.

"I don't know," said David. "Maybe there're Martians around we don't see. Sometimes nights I think I hear 'em. I hear the wind. The sand hits my window. I get scared. And I see those towns way up in the mountains where the Martians lived a long time ago. And I think I see things moving

---

B MOOD
Reread lines 15–26. On the basis of Bradbury's description of the **setting,** decide whether you have a positive or negative feeling about Mars. What words contribute to your feeling?

convivial
(kən-vĭv′ē-əl) *adj.*
enjoying the company of others; sociable

C READING SCIENCE FICTION
Reread lines 40–45. What are three examples of how Bradbury brings present-day life into this futuristic **setting?** Jot down these examples in your chart.

around those towns, Papa. And I wonder if those Martians *mind* us living
here. I wonder if they won't do something to us for coming here."

"Nonsense!" Mr. Bittering looked out the windows. "We're clean, decent
60 people." He looked at his children. "All dead cities have some kind of ghosts
in them. Memories, I mean." He stared at the hills. "You see a staircase and
you wonder what Martians looked like climbing it. You see Martian
paintings and you wonder what the painter was like. You make a little
ghost in your mind, a memory. It's quite natural. Imagination." He stopped.
"You haven't been prowling up in those ruins, have you?"

"No, Papa." David looked at his shoes.

"See that you stay away from them. Pass the jam."

"Just the same," said little David, "I bet something happens."

Something happened that afternoon. Laura stumbled through
70 the settlement, crying. She dashed blindly onto the porch.

"Mother, Father—the war, Earth!" she sobbed. "A radio flash just
came. Atom bombs[1] hit New York! All the space rockets blown up.
No more rockets to Mars, ever!"

"Oh, Harry!" The mother held onto her husband and daughter.

"Are you sure, Laura?" asked the father quietly.

Laura wept. "We're stranded on Mars, forever and ever!"

For a long time there was only the sound of the wind in the
late afternoon.

Alone, thought Bittering. Only a thousand of us here. No way back.
80 No way. No way. Sweat poured from his face and his hands and his
body; he was drenched in the hotness of his fear. He wanted to strike
Laura, cry, "No, you're lying! The rockets will come back!" Instead,
he stroked Laura's head against him and said, "The rockets will get
through someday." **D**

"Father, what will we do?"

"Go about our business, of course. Raise crops and children. Wait.
Keep things going until the war ends and the rockets come again."

The two boys stepped out onto the porch.

"Children," he said, sitting there, looking beyond them, "I've something
90 to tell you."

"We know," they said.

In the following days, Bittering wandered often through the garden
to stand alone in his fear. As long as the rockets had spun a silver web

Robotic equipment sent to Mars to gather data has shown that the planet has no signs of civilization, though there is some evidence of water on its surface.

D MOOD
Reread lines 79–84. Note that Bradbury uses sentence fragments to portray Bittering's thoughts. How does this help create a mood?

---

1. **atom bombs:** In 1945 the United States dropped atomic bombs over the cities of Hiroshima and Nagasaki, in Japan, killing over 100,000 people and injuring many thousands more.

across space, he had been able to accept Mars. For he had always told himself: Tomorrow, if I want, I can buy a ticket and go back to Earth.

But now: The web gone, the rockets lying in jigsaw heaps of molten girder and unsnaked wire. Earth people left to the strangeness of Mars, the cinnamon dusts and wine airs, to be baked like gingerbread shapes in Martian summers, put into harvested storage by Martian winters. What would happen to him, the others? This was the moment Mars had waited for. Now it would eat them.

He got down on his knees in the flower bed, a spade in his nervous hands. Work, he thought, work and forget.

He glanced up from the garden to the Martian mountains. He thought of the proud old Martian names that had once been on those peaks. Earthmen, dropping from the sky, had gazed upon hills, rivers, Martian seats left nameless in spite of names. Once Martians had built cities, named cities; climbed mountains, named mountains; sailed seas, named seas. Mountains melted, seas drained, cities tumbled. In spite of this, the Earthmen had felt a silent guilt at putting new names to these ancient hills and valleys. **E**

Nevertheless, man lives by symbol and label. The names were given.

Mr. Bittering felt very alone in his garden under the Martian sun, anachronism[2] bent here, planting Earth flowers in a wild soil.

Think. Keep thinking. Different things. Keep your mind free of Earth, the atom war, the lost rockets.

He perspired. He glanced about. No one watching. He removed his tie. Pretty bold, he thought. First your coat off, now your tie. He hung it neatly on a peach tree he had imported as a sapling from Massachusetts.

He returned to his philosophy of names and mountains. The Earthmen had changed names. Now there were Hormel Valleys, Roosevelt[3] Seas, Ford Hills, Vanderbilt Plateaus, Rockefeller[4] Rivers, on Mars. It wasn't right. The American settlers had shown wisdom, using old Indian prairie names: Wisconsin, Minnesota, Idaho, Ohio, Utah, Milwaukee, Waukegan, Osseo. The old names, the old meanings.

Staring at the mountains wildly, he thought: Are you up there? All the dead ones, you Martians? Well, here we are, alone, cut off! Come down, move us out! We're helpless!

The wind blew a shower of peach blossoms.

He put out his sun-browned hand and gave a small cry. He touched the blossoms and picked them up. He turned them, he touched them again and again. Then he shouted for his wife.

"Cora!"

She appeared at a window. He ran to her.

---

2. **anachronism** (ə-năk′rə-nĭz′əm): something placed outside of its proper time period.

3. **Roosevelt:** most likely refers to Franklin Delano Roosevelt, the 32nd president of the United States.

4. **Hormel … Ford … Vanderbilt … Rockefeller:** names of industrial and financial "giants" in American history.

Shellfish Flowers (1929), Max Ernst. Oil on canvas, 129 cm × 129 cm. Inv.: R 19 P. Photo Jean-Francois Tomasian. Musée National d'Art Moderne, Centre Georges Pompidou, Paris. © 2008 Artists Rights Society (ARS), New York/ADAGP, Paris.

"Cora, these blossoms!"

She handled them.

"Do you see? They're different. They've changed! They're not peach blossoms any more!"

"Look all right to me," she said.

"They're not. They're wrong! I can't tell how. An extra petal, a leaf,
140 something, the color, the smell!"

The children ran out in time to see their father hurrying about the garden, pulling up radishes, onions, and carrots from their beds.

"Cora, come look!"

They handled the onions, the radishes, the carrots among them.

"Do they look like carrots?"

"Yes . . . no." She hesitated. "I don't know."

"They're changed."

"Perhaps."

"You know they have! Onions but not onions, carrots but not carrots.
150 Taste: the same but different. Smell: not like it used to be." He felt his heart pounding, and he was afraid. He dug his fingers into the earth. "Cora, what's happening? What is it? We've got to get away from this." He ran across the garden. Each tree felt his touch. "The roses. The roses. They're turning green!" **F**

And they stood looking at the green roses.

And two days later Dan came running. "Come see the cow. I was milking her and I saw it. Come on!"

They stood in the shed and looked at their one cow.

It was growing a third horn.

160 And the lawn in front of their house very quietly and slowly was coloring itself like spring violets. Seed from Earth but growing up a soft purple.

"We must get away," said Bittering. "We'll eat this stuff and then we'll change—who knows to what? I can't let it happen. There's only one thing to do. Burn this food!" **G**

"It's not poisoned."

"But it is. **Subtly,** very subtly. A little bit. A very little bit. We mustn't touch it."

He looked with dismay at their house. "Even the house. The wind's done something to it. The air's burned it. The fog at night. The boards, 170 all warped out of shape. It's not an Earthman's house any more."

"Oh, your imagination!"

He put on his coat and tie. "I'm going into town. We've got to do something now. I'll be back."

"Wait, Harry!" his wife cried. But he was gone.

In town, on the shadowy step of the grocery store, the men sat with their hands on their knees, conversing with great leisure and ease.

Mr. Bittering wanted to fire a pistol in the air.

What are you doing, you fools! he thought. Sitting here! You've heard the news—we're stranded on this planet. Well, move! Aren't you 180 frightened? Aren't you afraid? What are you going to do?

"Hello, Harry," said everyone.

"Look," he said to them. "You did hear the news, the other day, didn't you?"

They nodded and laughed. "Sure. Sure, Harry."

"What are you going to do about it?"

"Do, Harry, do? What *can* we do?"

"Build a rocket, that's what!"

"A rocket, Harry? To go back to all that trouble? Oh, Harry!"

"But you *must* want to go back. Have you noticed the peach blossoms, 190 the onions, the grass?"

"Why, yes, Harry, seems we did," said one of the men.

"Doesn't it scare you?"

"Can't recall that it did much, Harry." **H**

"Idiots!"

"Now, Harry."

Bittering wanted to cry. "You've got to work with me. If we stay here, we'll all change. The air. Don't you smell it? Something in the air. A Martian virus, maybe; some seed, or a pollen. Listen to me!"

They stared at him.

"Sam," he said to one of them.

"Yes, Harry?"

"Will you help me build a rocket?"

"Harry, I got a whole load of metal and some blueprints. You want to work in my metal shop on a rocket, you're welcome. I'll sell you that metal for five hundred dollars. You should be able to construct a right pretty rocket, if you work alone, in about thirty years."

Everyone laughed.

"Don't laugh."

Sam looked at him with quiet good humor.

"Sam," Bittering said. "Your eyes—"

"What about them, Harry?"

"Didn't they used to be gray?"

"Well now, I don't remember."

"They were, weren't they?"

"Why do you ask, Harry?"

"Because now they're kind of yellow-colored."

"Is that so, Harry?" Sam said, casually.

"And you're taller and thinner—"

"You might be right, Harry."

"Sam, you shouldn't have yellow eyes." **I**

"Harry, what color eyes have *you* got?" Sam said.

"My eyes? They're blue, of course."

"Here you are, Harry." Sam handed him a pocket mirror. "Take a look at yourself."

Mr. Bittering hesitated, and then raised the mirror to his face.

There were little, very dim flecks of new gold captured in the blue of his eyes.

"Now look what you've done," said Sam a moment later. "You've broken my mirror." **J**

Harry Bittering moved into the metal shop and began to build the rocket. Men stood in the open door and talked and joked without raising their voices. Once in a while they gave him a hand on lifting something. But mostly they just idled and watched him with their yellowing eyes.

"It's suppertime, Harry," they said.

His wife appeared with his supper in a wicker basket.

"I won't touch it," he said. "I'll eat only food from our Deepfreeze. Food that came from Earth. Nothing from our garden."

His wife stood watching him. "You can't build a rocket."

240 "I worked in a shop once, when I was twenty. I know metal. Once I get it started, the others will help," he said, not looking at her, laying out the blueprints.

"Harry, Harry," she said, helplessly.

"We've *got* to get away, Cora. We've got to!"

The nights were full of wind that blew down the empty moonlit sea meadows past the little white chess cities lying for their twelve-thousandth year in the shallows. In the Earthmen's settlement, the Bittering house shook with a feeling of change.

Lying abed, Mr. Bittering felt his bones shifted, shaped, melted like gold.
250 His wife, lying beside him, was dark from many sunny afternoons. Dark she was, and golden-eyed, burnt almost black by the sun, sleeping, and the children metallic in their beds, and the wind roaring **forlorn** and changing through the old peach trees, the violet grass, shaking out green rose petals. **K**

The fear would not be stopped. It had his throat and heart. It dripped in a wetness of the arm and the temple and the trembling palm.

A green star rose in the east.

A strange word emerged from Mr. Bittering's lips.

"Iorrt. Iorrt." He repeated it.

260 It was a Martian word. He knew no Martian.

In the middle of the night he arose and dialed a call through to Simpson, the archaeologist.

"Simpson, what does the word *Iorrt* mean?"

"Why that's the old Martian word for our planet Earth. Why?"

K MOOD

Reread lines 245–253. Notice the language Bradbury uses to describe the setting and characters. Writers use language that will help the reader sense the feeling of a scene. In addition, notice the sentence structure, such as "Dark she was . . . " What mood do these elements create?

forlorn (fər-lôrn′) *adj.* appearing lonely or sad

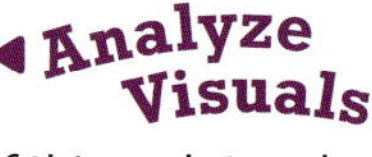

◄**Analyze Visuals**

If this sculpture had been made specifically for this story, which figure would represent Harry?

The Forest (1950), Alberto Giacometti. Bronze, painted, 22" x 24" x 19 1/4". Gift of Enid Haupt. National Gallery of Art, Washington, D.C. © National Gallery of Art, Washington, D.C. © 2008 Artists Rights Society (ARS), New York/ADAGP, Paris.

"No special reason."

270   The telephone slipped from his hand.

"Hello, hello, hello, hello," it kept saying while he sat gazing out at the green star. "Bittering? Harry, are you there?"

The days were full of metal sound. He laid the frame of the rocket with the reluctant help of three indifferent men. He grew very tired in an hour or so and had to sit down. ◆

"The altitude," laughed a man.

"Are you *eating*, Harry?" asked another.

"I'm eating," he said, angrily.

"From your Deepfreeze?"

280   "Yes!"

"You're getting thinner, Harry."

"I'm not!"

"And taller."

"Liar!"

His wife took him aside a few days later. "Harry, I've used up all the food in the Deepfreeze. There's nothing left. I'll have to make sandwiches using food grown on Mars."

He sat down heavily.

"You must eat," she said. "You're weak."

290   "Yes," he said.

He took a sandwich, opened it, looked at it, and began to nibble at it.

"And take the rest of the day off," she said. "It's hot. The children want to swim in the canals and hike. Please come along."

"I can't waste time. This is a crisis!"

"Just for an hour," she urged. "A swim'll do you good."

He rose, sweating. "All right, all right. Leave me alone. I'll come."

"Good for you, Harry."

The sun was hot, the day quiet. There was only an immense staring burn upon the land. They moved along the canal, the father, the mother,

300 the racing children in their swimsuits. They stopped and ate meat sandwiches. He saw their skin baking brown. And he saw the yellow eyes of his wife and his children, their eyes that were never yellow before. A few tremblings shook him, but were carried off in waves of pleasant heat as he lay in the sun. He was too tired to be afraid. ●

"Cora, how long have your eyes been yellow?"

She was bewildered. "Always, I guess."

"They didn't change from brown in the last three months?"

She bit her lips. "No. Why do you ask?"

"Never mind."

◆ GRAMMAR IN CONTEXT

In lines 274–275, notice how Bradbury uses the prepositional phrase, *in an hour or so.* The verb that follows the phrase agrees with the subject, *He.*

● MOOD

Reread lines 301–304. Note how different Harry's attitude is now than it was before. What effect does this change have on you as a reader?

310 They sat there.

"The children's eyes," he said. "They're yellow, too."

"Sometimes growing children's eyes change color."

"Maybe *we're* children, too. At least to Mars. That's a thought."
He laughed. "Think I'll swim."

They leaped into the canal water, and he let himself sink down and
down to the bottom like a golden statue and lie there in green silence.
All was water-quiet and deep, all was peace. He felt the steady, slow
current drift him easily.

If I lie here long enough, he thought, the water will work and eat away
320 my flesh until the bones show like coral. Just my skeleton left. And then
the water can build on that skeleton—green things, deep water things,
red things, yellow things. Change. Change. Slow, deep, silent change.
And isn't that what it is up *there*?

He saw the sky submerged above him, the sun made Martian by
atmosphere and time and space.

Up there, a big river, he thought, a Martian river; all of us lying deep
in it, in our pebble houses, in our sunken boulder houses, like crayfish
hidden, and the water washing away our old bodies and lengthening the
bones and—
330 He let himself drift up through the soft light.

Dan sat on the edge of the canal, regarding his father seriously.

"*Utha,*" he said.

"What?" asked his father.

The boy smiled. "You know. *Utha's* the Martian word for 'father.'"

"Where did you learn it?"

"I don't know. Around. *Utha!*"

"What do you want?"

The boy hesitated. "I—I want to change my name."

"Change it?"
340 "Yes."

His mother swam over. "What's wrong with Dan for a name?"

Dan fidgeted. "The other day you called Dan, Dan, Dan. I didn't
even hear. I said to myself, That's not my name. I've a new name I want
to use."

Mr. Bittering held to the side of the canal, his body cold and his heart
pounding slowly. "What is this new name?"

"Linnl. Isn't that a good name? Can I use it? Can't I, please?" Ⓜ

Mr. Bittering put his hand to his head. He thought of the silly rocket,
himself working alone, himself alone even among his family, so alone.
350 He heard his wife say, "Why not?"

He heard himself say, "Yes, you can use it."

"Yaaa!" screamed the boy. "I'm Linnl, Linnl!"

Ⓜ **MAKE INFERENCES**
Why does Dan want to change his name?

Racing down the meadowlands, he danced and shouted.

Mr. Bittering looked at his wife. "Why did we do that?"

"I don't know," she said. "It just seemed like a good idea."

They walked into the hills. They strolled on old mosaic paths, beside still pumping fountains. The paths were covered with a thin film of cool water all summer long. You kept your bare feet cool all the day, splashing as in a creek, wading.

360   They came to a small deserted Martian villa with a good view of the valley. It was on top of a hill. Blue marble halls, large murals, a swimming pool. It was refreshing in this hot summertime. The Martians hadn't believed in large cities.

"How nice," said Mrs. Bittering, "if we could move up here to this villa for the summer."

"Come on," he said. "We're going back to town. There's work to be done on the rocket."

But as he worked that night, the thought of the cool blue marble villa entered his mind. As the hours passed, the rocket seemed

370 less important. **N**

In the flow of days and weeks, the rocket **receded** and **dwindled.** The old fever was gone. It frightened him to think he had let it slip this way. But somehow the heat, the air, the working conditions—

He heard the men murmuring on the porch of his metal shop.

"Everyone's going. You heard?"

"All going. That's right."

Bittering came out. "Going where?" He saw a couple of trucks, loaded with children and furniture, drive down the dusty street.

"Up to the villas," said the man.

380   "Yeah, Harry. I'm going. So is Sam. Aren't you Sam?"

"That's right, Harry. What about you?"

"I've got work to do here."

"Work! You can finish that rocket in the autumn, when it's cooler."

He took a breath. "I got the frame all set up."

"In the autumn is better." Their voices were lazy in the heat.

"Got to work," he said.

"Autumn," they reasoned. And they sounded so sensible, so right.

"Autumn would be best," he thought. "Plenty of time, then."

No! cried part of himself, deep down, put away, locked tight,

390 suffocating. No! No!

"In the autumn," he said.

"Come on, Harry," they all said.

"Yes," he said, feeling his flesh melt in the hot liquid air. "Yes, in the autumn. I'll begin work again then."

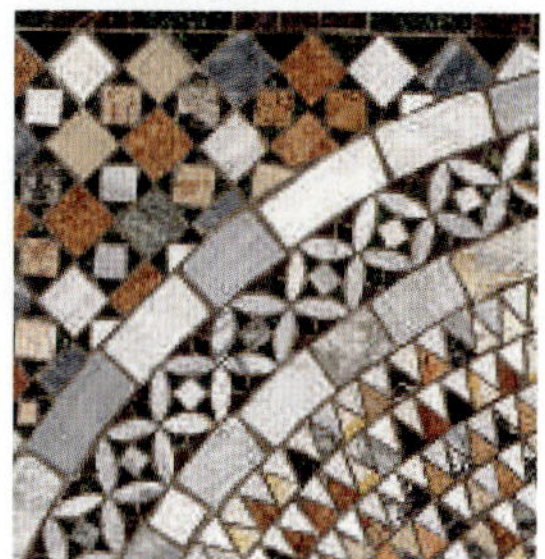

mosaic (mō-zā′ĭk) *adj.* formed from pieces of stone or glass that are inlaid to make a design

N **MAKE INFERENCES**
Why is the rocket becoming less important to Harry?

recede (rĭ-sēd′) *v.* to become fainter or more distant

dwindle (dwĭn′dl) *v.* to become less, until little remains

Detail from *Figures Crossing River on Gold Coins*, Andrew Judd. ©Andrew Judd/Masterfile.

"I got a villa near the Tirra Canal," said someone.

"You mean the Roosevelt Canal, don't you?"

"Tirra. The old Martian name."

"But on the map—"

"Forget the map. It's Tirra now. Now I found a place in the Pillan
400 Mountains—"

"You mean the Rockefeller Range," said Bittering.

"I mean the Pillan Mountains," said Sam.

"Yes," said Bittering, buried in the hot, swarming air. "The Pillan
Mountains."

Everyone worked at loading the truck in the hot, still afternoon
of the next day.

Laura, Dan, and David carried packages. Or, as they preferred
to be known, Ttil, Linnl, and Werr carried packages. 🅞

The furniture was abandoned in the little white cottage.

410 "It looked just fine in Boston," said the mother. "And here
in the cottage. But up at the villa? No. We'll get it when we come
back in the autumn."

Bittering himself was quiet.

"I've some ideas on furniture for the villa," he said after a time.
"Big, lazy furniture."

"What about your encyclopedia? You're taking it along, surely?"

Mr. Bittering glanced away. "I'll come and get it next week."

They turned to their daughter. "What about your New York dresses?"

The bewildered girl stared. "Why, I don't want them any more."

420 They shut off the gas, the water, they locked the doors and walked away. Father peered into the truck.

"Gosh, we're not taking much," he said. "Considering all we brought to Mars, this is only a handful!" ⓟ

He started the truck.

Looking at the small white cottage for a long moment, he was filled with a desire to rush to it, touch it, say good-bye to it, for he felt as if he were going away on a long journey, leaving something to which he could never quite return, never understand again.

Just then Sam and his family drove by in another truck.

430 "Hi, Bittering! Here we go!"

The truck swung down the ancient highway out of town. There were sixty others traveling in the same direction. The town filled with a silent, heavy dust from their passage. The canal waters lay blue in the sun, and a quiet wind moved in the strange trees.

"Good-bye, town!" said Mr. Bittering.

"Good-bye, good-bye," said the family, waving to it.

They did not look back again.

Summer burned the canals dry. Summer moved like flame upon the meadows. In the empty Earth settlement, the painted houses flaked
440 and peeled. Rubber tires upon which children had swung in back yards hung suspended like stopped clock **pendulums** in the blazing air.

At the metal shop, the rocket frame began to rust.

In the quiet autumn Mr. Bittering stood, very dark now, very golden-eyed, upon the slope above his villa, looking at the valley.

"It's time to go back," said Cora.

"Yes, but we're not going," he said quietly. "There's nothing there any more."

"Your books," she said. "Your fine clothes."

"Your *llles* and your fine *ior uele rre,*" she said.

450 "The town's empty. No one's going back," he said. "There's no reason to, none at all."

The daughter wove tapestries and the sons played songs on ancient flutes and pipes, their laughter echoing in the marble villa.

Mr. Bittering gazed at the Earth settlement far away in the low valley. "Such odd, such ridiculous houses the Earth people built."

"They didn't know any better," his wife **mused.** "Such ugly people. I'm glad they've gone."

They both looked at each other, startled by all they had just finished
saying. They laughed.

460 "Where did they go?" he wondered. He glanced at his wife. She was
golden and slender as his daughter. She looked at him, and he seemed
almost as young as their eldest son. **Q**

"I don't know," she said.

"We'll go back to town maybe next year, or the year after, or the year
after that," he said, calmly. "Now—I'm warm. How about taking a swim?"

They turned their backs to the valley. Arm in arm they walked silently
down a path of clear-running spring water.

470 Five years later a rocket fell out of the sky. It lay steaming in the
valley. Men leaped out of it, shouting.

"We won the war on Earth! We're here to rescue you! Hey!"

But the American-built town of cottages, peach trees, and theaters was
silent. They found a **flimsy** rocket frame rusting in an empty shop.

The rocket men searched the hills. The captain established
headquarters in an abandoned bar. His lieutenant came back to report.

"The town's empty, but we found native life in the hills, sir. Dark
people. Yellow eyes. Martians. Very friendly. We talked a bit, not much.
They learn English fast. I'm sure our relations will be most friendly with
them, sir."

"Dark, eh?" mused the captain. "How many?"

480 "Six, eight hundred, I'd say, living in those marble ruins in the hills,
sir. Tall, healthy. Beautiful women."

"Did they tell you what became of the men and women who built
this Earth settlement, Lieutenant?"

"They hadn't the foggiest notion of what happened to this town
or its people."

"Strange. You think those Martians killed them?"

"They look surprisingly peaceful. Chances are a plague did this
town in, sir."

"Perhaps. I suppose this is one of those mysteries we'll never solve.
490 One of those mysteries you read about." **R**

The captain looked at the room, the dusty windows, the blue mountains
rising beyond, the canals moving in the light, and he heard the soft wind
in the air. He shivered. Then, recovering, he tapped a large fresh map he
had thumbtacked to the top of an empty table.

"Lots to be done, Lieutenant." His voice droned on and quietly on as
the sun sank behind the blue hills. "New settlements. Mining sites, minerals
to be looked for. Bacteriological specimens⁵ taken. The work, all the work.

---

5. **bacteriological specimens:** samples of different kinds of single-celled living things.

Q READING SCIENCE FICTION
Reread lines 460–462.
Find details that tell you
how the Bitterings have
changed since they first
arrived on Mars. Are
they still human?

flimsy (flĭm′zē) *adj.*
not solid or strong

R MAKE INFERENCES
What do you think will
happen to the captain
and the lieutenant?

The Whole City (1935), Max Ernst. Oil on canvas, 60 cm × 81 cm. Kunsthaus, Zurich, Switzerland. © 2008 Artists Rights Society (ARS), New York/ADAGP, Paris.

And the old records were lost. We'll have a job of remapping to do, renaming the mountains and rivers and such. Calls for a little imagination.

"What do you think of naming those mountains the Lincoln Mountains, this canal the Washington Canal, those hills—we can name those hills for you, Lieutenant. Diplomacy. And you, for a favor, might name a town for me. Polishing the apple.[6] And why not make this the Einstein Valley, and farther over . . . are you *listening,* Lieutenant?"

The lieutenant snapped his gaze from the blue color and the quiet mist of the hills far beyond the town.

"What? Oh, *yes,* sir!" ❧

Does the place at the top of the hill look inviting to you? Why or why not?

---

6. **polishing the apple:** acting in a way to get on the good side of another person.

NEWSPAPER ARTICLE As you read this interview, you'll find out how Ray Bradbury views himself as an author, how he writes stories like "Dark They Were, and Golden-Eyed," and what advice he has for beginning writers.

Section 3   THE CHARLOTTE OBSERVER   C3

An Interview with
RAY BRADBURY

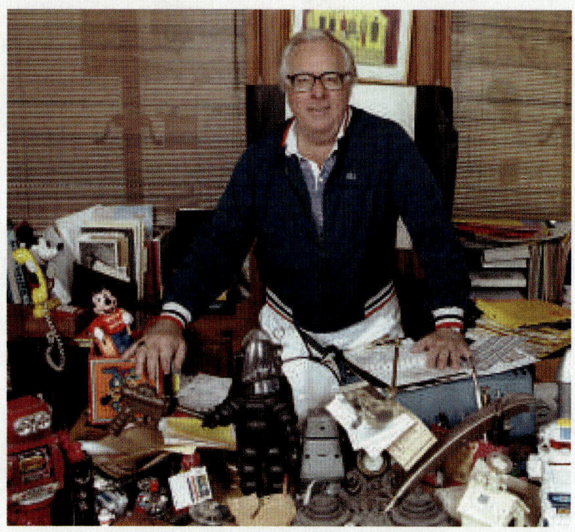

Q: You don't consider yourself a science fiction writer, even though others call you that. How do you see yourself?

A: I am a collector of metaphors. Any idea that strikes me I run with. . . .

I wrote *The October Country,* which is weird fantasy. There is no science fiction there. And *Halloween Tree,* which is a history of Halloween. And *Dandelion Wine,* which is my childhood in Illinois. *Something Wicked This Way Comes,* which is also my childhood plus fantasy. So when you look at the spread of things, there is only one novel that is science fiction. And that's *Fahrenheit 451.* In other words, science fiction is the art of the possible, not the art of the impossible. As soon as you deal with things that can't happen you are writing fantasy.

Q: Walk me through your daily inspiration and writing process.

A: I just wake up with ideas every morning from my subconscious percolating. At 7 in the morning I lie in bed and I watch all the fragments of ideas swarming around in my head and these voices talk to me. And when they get to a certain point, I jump out of bed and run to the typewriter. So I'm not in control. Two hours later I have a new short story or an essay or part of a play. . . .

Q: What kind of advice would you give beginning writers?

A: Explode. Don't intellectualize. Get passionate about ideas. Cram your head full of images. Stay in the library. Stay off the Internet. Read all the great books. Read all the great poetry. See all the great films. Fill your life with metaphors. And then explode. And you're bound to do something good.

Comprehension

1. **Recall** Why do the Bitterings settle on Mars?

2. **Recall** Why do the rockets from Earth stop coming to Mars?

3. **Represent** Create a timeline of the main events of the story, including the physical changes Harry notices in the people and things around him.

Text Analysis

4. **Identify Mood** Before you read the story, you were asked to consider, as you read, how Bradbury's choice of words affected the way you felt. Now think of the story as a whole. What words would you use to describe the overall mood of the story? Cite examples of Bradbury's use of language to support your response.

5. **Analyze Science Fiction** Although this story was originally published in 1949, some of Bradbury's comments about life in the real world or about human nature still ring true. In portraying human life on Mars, what do you think Bradbury was saying about human nature?

6. **Analyze Character** Harry changes throughout the story. Using an organizer like the one shown, record his attitude and appearance at the beginning, middle, and end of the story.

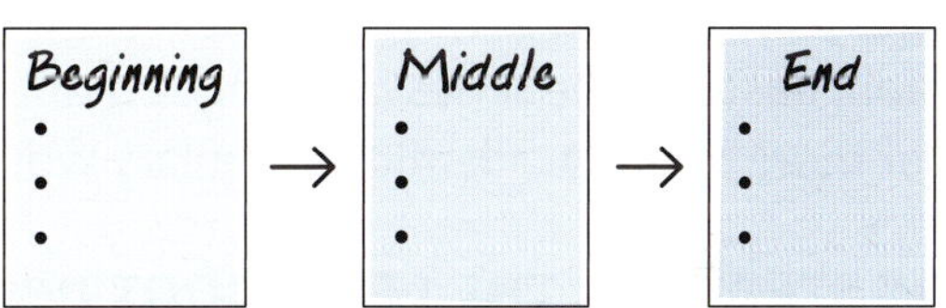

7. **Make Inferences** Who do you think will resist change the most, the captain or the lieutenant? Use examples from the story to support your answer.

8. **Evaluate Science Fiction** Reread Bradbury's first answer from the interview on page 478. Note that he does not consider himself a science fiction writer. In light of this information, do you think it is right to label "Dark They Were, and Golden-Eyed" as science fiction? Explain your answer, using support from the selection, the chart you created as you read, and the interview.

Extension and Challenge

9. **SCIENCE CONNECTION** Find out more about Mars by visiting the library in your school or neighborhood. What do we now know about the planet? What plans are scientists making to study it further? Focus your research on what interests you most. Report your findings to the class.

Can where you are **CHANGE** who you are?

Recall the chart you created on page 460. Now that you've read about the experience of the Bittering family, have you changed your mind about how a place might change you? Explain.

Vocabulary in Context

▲ VOCABULARY PRACTICE

Write the letter of the phrase that has a connection to each vocabulary word.

1. **pendulum: (a)** a grandfather clock, **(b)** a racing motorcycle, **(c)** a gossiping man
2. **forlorn: (a)** a heavy snowfall, **(b)** a bitter quarrel, **(c)** a lonely child
3. **dwindle: (a)** your supply of money, **(b)** your age, **(c)** your science textbook
4. **subtly: (a)** a fireworks show, **(b)** a gradually dimming light, **(c)** a long bus ride
5. **convivial: (a)** a dog and a squirrel, **(b)** a friendly crowd, **(c)** a curving staircase
6. **flimsy: (a)** a stuffed chair, **(b)** a weak argument, **(c)** a party in a yard
7. **recede: (a)** a plane flying away, **(b)** an arriving plane, **(c)** a plane parked at a gate
8. **muse: (a)** a noisy band, **(b)** a person considering choices, **(c)** a windy day

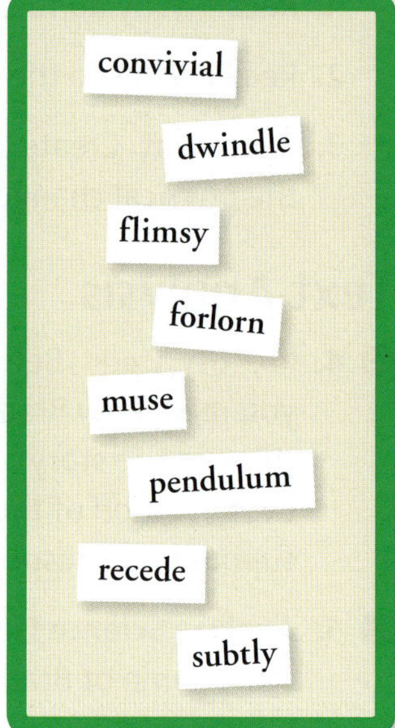

ACADEMIC VOCABULARY IN WRITING

• communicate   • describe   • illustrate   • interpret   • style

In a paragraph, **describe** the series of changes that affect the Bitterings. Try to use one or more of the Academic Vocabulary words in your paragraph.

VOCABULARY STRATEGY: THE LATIN ROOT *pend*

The vocabulary word *pendulum* contains the Latin root *pend*, which means "hang." This root, which is sometimes spelled *pens*, is found in many English words. To understand the meaning of words with *pend or pens*, use context clues and your knowledge of the root's meaning.

L 4b Use Latin roots as clues to the meaning of a word.

PRACTICE Choose the word from the web that best completes each sentence. Then explain how the root *pend* relates to the meaning of the word.

1. She wears that _______ around her neck every day.
2. My choice is _______ on what you decide to do.
3. The book was so _______ that he couldn't stop reading it.
4. To hold up his pants, Dad prefers _______ to belts.
5. They could not shake off their feeling of _______ trouble.

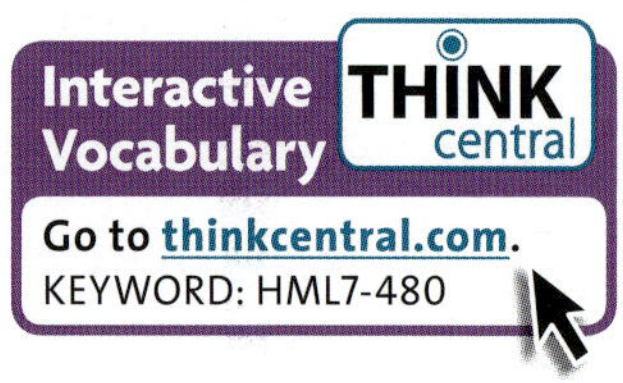

Language

◆ GRAMMAR IN CONTEXT: Understand Prepositions

Review the **Grammar in Context** note on page 471. In all types of sentences, a verb must **agree in number** with its subject. **Number** refers to whether a word is singular or plural. A **prepositional phrase** is a group of words that begins with a preposition, such as *from, in, under,* or *with,* and ends with a noun or pronoun. Be especially careful when you form a sentence that has a **prepositional phrase** between the subject and the verb. In cases like these, the number of the subject is not changed by the phrase that follows the subject.

> *Original:* Harry, under the circumstances, struggle to cope.
>
> *Revised:* Harry, under the circumstances, struggles to cope.
> (*The subject* Harry *is singular so the verb should be too.*)

PRACTICE Choose the verb form that agrees in number with each subject.

1. Humans from around the world (wonder, wonders) about life on Mars.
2. Cora Bittering, with much patience, (try, tries) to understand her husband.
3. Harry, apart from the others, (resist, resists) the peculiar changes.
4. Eventually, Harry, along with the others, (move, moves) to the Martian villas.

For more help with subject-verb agreement, see pages R65–R67 in the **Grammar Handbook**.

READING-WRITING CONNECTION

Increase your understanding of "Dark They Were, and Golden-Eyed" by responding to this prompt. Then use the **revising tip** to improve your writing.

WRITING PROMPT	REVISING TIP
Short Constructed Response: Letter Bradbury originally named "Dark They Were, and Golden-Eyed" "The Naming of Names." Which title do you think is more appropriate? Using details and examples from the story, write a **one-paragraph letter** to the author to explain your choice.	Review your response. Do the subjects and verbs agree in number? If not, revise your writing.

COMMON CORE

L 1a Explain the function of phrases in specific sentences.
W 3 Write narratives to develop real or imagined experiences or events.

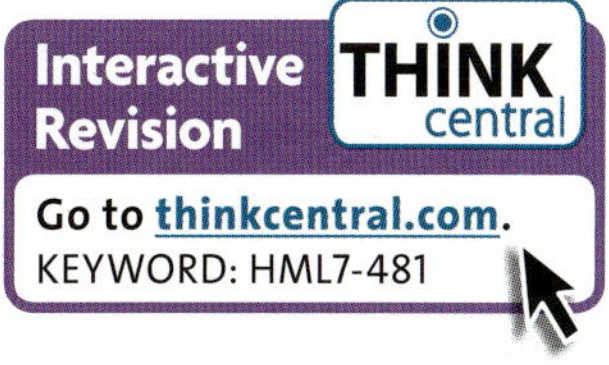

Reading for Information

In today's information age, knowledge is power. Facts and figures on just about any subject, from consumer products to Jupiter's moons, are at your fingertips. How do you find the information you're looking for in expository texts? What are the best ways to understand and remember what you read? By paying attention to the structure, purpose, and organization of informational texts, you will more fully comprehend what you read.

COMMON CORE

Included in this workshop:
RI 1 Cite textual evidence to support analysis of what the text says explicitly. **RI 2** Determine central ideas in a text; provide an objective summary. **RI 5** Analyze the structure an author uses to organize a text.

Part 1: Text Features and Graphic Aids

Flipping through a newspaper or surfing the Web for information can be an overwhelming experience. To help readers get their bearings and quickly see what a text is about, many writers use **text features,** or special design elements. Text features include headings, subheadings, boldfaced type, and captions. These elements all serve as road signs, guiding you through a text and pointing out key ideas.

Just as you would look at a road map before driving to a new place, you may find it helpful to **preview** a text before you start to read it. Notice how much you can tell about this textbook article by scanning the text features.

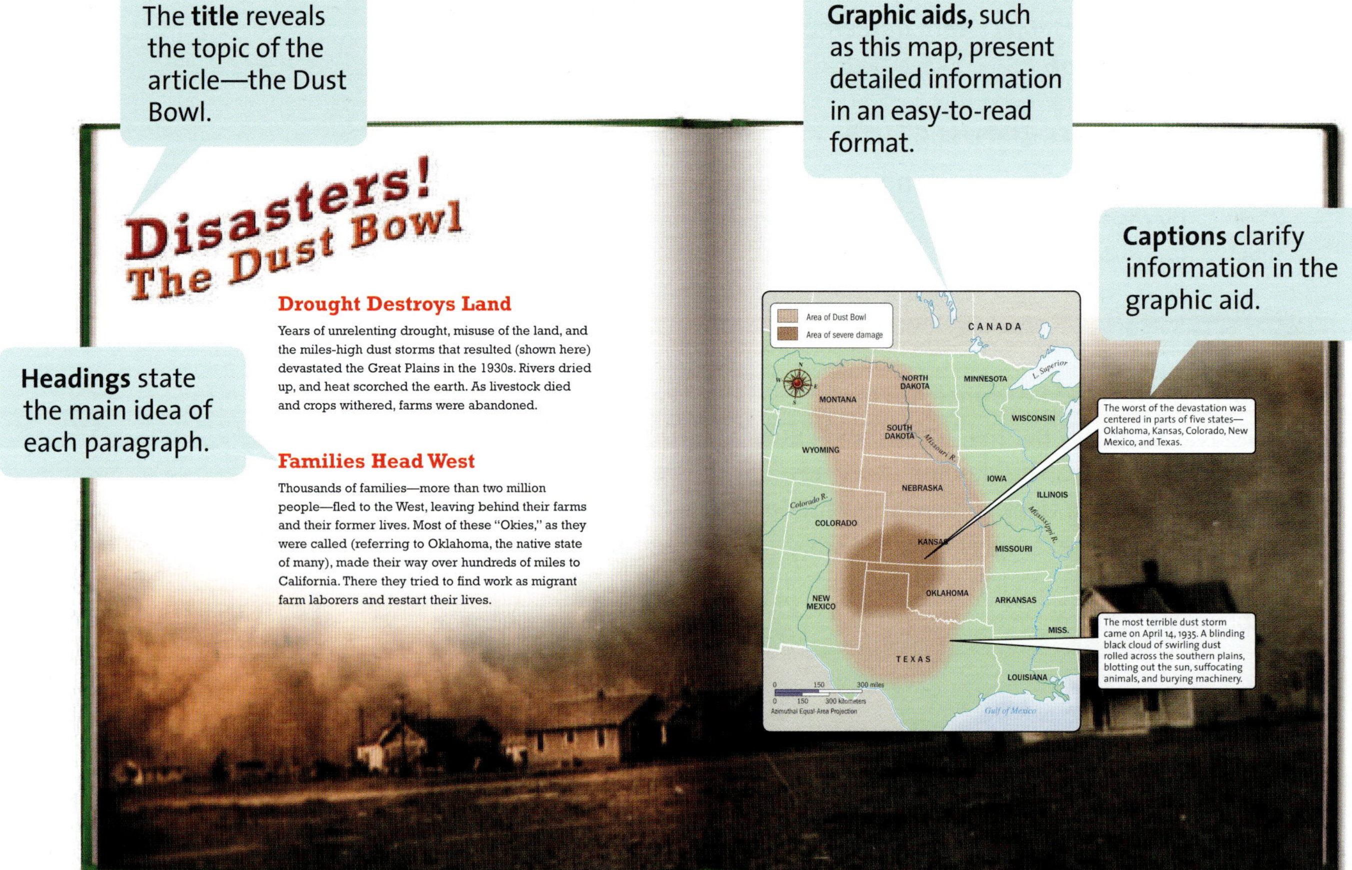

Quickly skim the text features of this article. After seeing these features, what information do you think the article will provide? Now read the passage closely and answer the questions.

from

EARTHQUAKES

Reference article in **Popular Science Almanac**

    . . . Earth's crust isn't just one solid piece, like an eggshell. Instead, it's broken up into different pieces, called plates. . . .

5   . . . Plate movement is responsible for earthquakes as well as volcanoes. See, Earth's plates are constantly growing at one end, getting consumed at the other, shifting alongside other

10 plates, and pushing headlong into others. All of this causes a tremendous amount of pressure build-up. Rocks are rigid. Since they don't break easily, they resist this pressure for a long,

15 long time. But after a while, something's got to give. Rapid movement of massive blocks of rock releases the tension . . . at least for the time being.

The San Andreas Fault in California falls at the boundary of two tectonic plates. The slipping of these plates is often the cause of earthquakes in the region.

Anatomy of an Earthquake

Close Read

1. An **almanac** is an annual reference book. Its purpose is to publish brief articles relating to a specific field. If you were doing a report on the parts of an earthquake, would this almanac article help you? Explain your answer.

2. Name two things you learn about earthquakes from the caption and the photograph.

3. Review the graphic aid at the bottom of this article. In your own words, describe the information it presents.

Part 2: Use Organizational Patterns

Text features may be the road signs guiding you through a text, but your final destination is an understanding of what you've read. The following strategies can help you reach that destination.

IDENTIFY THE MAIN IDEAS

Main ideas, or **central ideas,** are the most important ideas about a topic that a writer wants to communicate to readers. **Supporting details,** such as facts and examples, help to explain or elaborate on the main ideas. Most of the time, the main idea of a paragraph is directly stated in a **topic sentence,** which is usually located at the beginning or end of that paragraph. Consider this example from the article you just read.

> . . . Plate movement is responsible for earthquakes as well as volcanoes. See, Earth's plates are constantly growing at one end, getting consumed at the other, shifting alongside other plates, and pushing headlong into others. . . .

This **topic sentence** states the main idea of one paragraph in the article: the cause of earthquakes.

This **supporting detail** further explains what plate movement is and how it can cause earthquakes.

If the main idea is **implied**—suggested but not directly stated—you have to **infer** it by asking yourself: What do the supporting details add up to?

To clearly communicate their ideas, writers usually organize an entire text in a pattern. One of the most basic **patterns of organization** for an expository text is main idea and supporting details, in which a central idea about a topic is presented and then supported by details. There are many other organizational patterns that communicate a text's important ideas and details, including cause and effect and chronological order. You can use any of these organizational patterns as guides to help you form an overview of a text and **summarize** it, which is to briefly retell a text's main ideas in your own words.

TAKE NOTES

When you take notes, you zero in on the main ideas and supporting details and restate them in your own words. You can take notes by setting up a **graphic organizer** or an **outline** that you can follow easily. For example, to create a formal outline like this one, use Roman numerals to label the main ideas, capital letters to label the supporting points, and Arabic numerals to label supporting details.

Earthquakes

I. Caused by movement of plates
(pieces of the earth's crust)

   A. Plates hit each other.

   B. Movement causes pressure
      on rocks.

   C. Tension is released when
      rock shifts.

II. Anatomy of an earthquake

   A. Focus is the point where
      rock shifts underground.

   B. Epicenter is the point on
      surface above focus.

Part 3: Analyze the Text

Read this article about the *Titanic,* the famous ship that sank in 1912. Preview the article and answer the first **Close Read** question. Then read the article more closely, using the other questions to help you take notes.

SCIENCE WATCH

What's Eating the *Titanic?*

The world's most famous sunken wreck becomes a gift for deep-sea scientists.

Oceanographer Robert Ballard is returning to the *Titanic,* but it's not the same sunken ship he found in 1985. The deep ocean has been steadily destroying the once-great cruise liner, and scientists say the process is unlike any they've ever seen. "Even if we could stop it, I wouldn't," says scientist Charles Pellegrino. "The *Titanic* is becoming something that belongs to biology."

The ship has attracted all kinds of hungry deep-sea life. Other critters (including tourists) are steadily chomping away at the ship too. Here's your guide to the wreck's undoing.

THE CULPRITS	THE DESTRUCTION	AN END IN SIGHT?
Mollusks and microorganisms that stirred up from the ocean floor when the ship first hit bottom	Worms munched on softer woods, while microorganisms ate some clothes and other fabrics. By the time scientists arrived to survey the ship, only the hard woods, such as mahogony, remained.	The worms moved on—the worst is done.
Bacteria from the ocean floor	Living off the sulfur in steel, bacteria also remove iron for housing and get rid of the rest. Bacteria have sucked over 1,000 tons of iron from the ship.	The bacterial colonies are growing, and half the steel could be gone by 2204.
The elements, such as water pressure, salt, and icebergs	Water pressure damaged parts of the ship when it sank. Salt slowly eats away at the hull, while gravel from icebergs overhead rains down on the deck.	Some suggest saving specific parts of the *Titanic* by bringing them on shore.
Tourists, pirates, and explorers attracted by profit and the popularity of *Titanic* TV specials	Small submarines are used to explore the site of the wreck. Careless piloting of these submarines has caused some damage to the hull and the deck.	The government has rules for protecting sunken ships, but it does not have the power to enforce them.

Close Read

1. Preview the title, the subtitle, and the headings in the chart. What do you think this article will be about?

2. The main idea of the first paragraph is listed in the outline shown. In your notebook, record two supporting details.

I. Scientists see the Titanic's destruction as an opportunity for study.
A.
B.

3. The second paragraph and the chart present another main idea listed by Roman numeral II. One supporting detail has been filled in. Complete the outline by adding other details.

II. Many culprits are causing the destruction.
A. Mollusks and microorganisms
1. Worms ate softer woods.
2. Microorganisms ate fabrics.
3. Worst damage is done.

Argument and Persuasion

Have you ever tried to count the number of persuasive messages you see and hear each day? Letters to the editor, billboards, slogans on the back of your cereal box—persuasive messages are everywhere. In this workshop, you will learn how to analyze the arguments at the heart of these messages and recognize the techniques that are used to persuade you. Armed with this knowledge, you can make up your own mind about messages and ideas that matter.

COMMON CORE

Included in this workshop:
RI 4 Determine the meaning of words and phrases as they are used in a text; analyze the impact of word choice. **RI 5** Analyze the structure an author uses to organize a text. **RI 8** Trace and evaluate the argument and specific claims in a text, assessing whether the reasoning is sound.

Part 1: What Is an Argument?

When you hear the word *argument,* you might think of a fight between two people, complete with differences of opinion, angry shouting, and hurt feelings. In formal speaking and writing, however, an argument is not emotional. It is a claim supported by reasons and evidence.

A **claim** is a writer's position on a problem or an issue. A claim might be stated directly, as in this example: "Crunchy Puffs are an important part of a nutritious breakfast." Sometimes a writer's claim is implied, as in this slogan: "Juan for Student Council—Let the Good Times Roll." The slogan suggests that if Juan is elected, everyone at school will have more fun.

The strength of an argument depends not on the claim but on the **support,** or the reasons and evidence that are used to prove the claim. It is important to evaluate the adequacy, accuracy, and appropriateness of the evidence, which can include facts, statistics, and examples.

Look closely at the elements of an argument in this example.

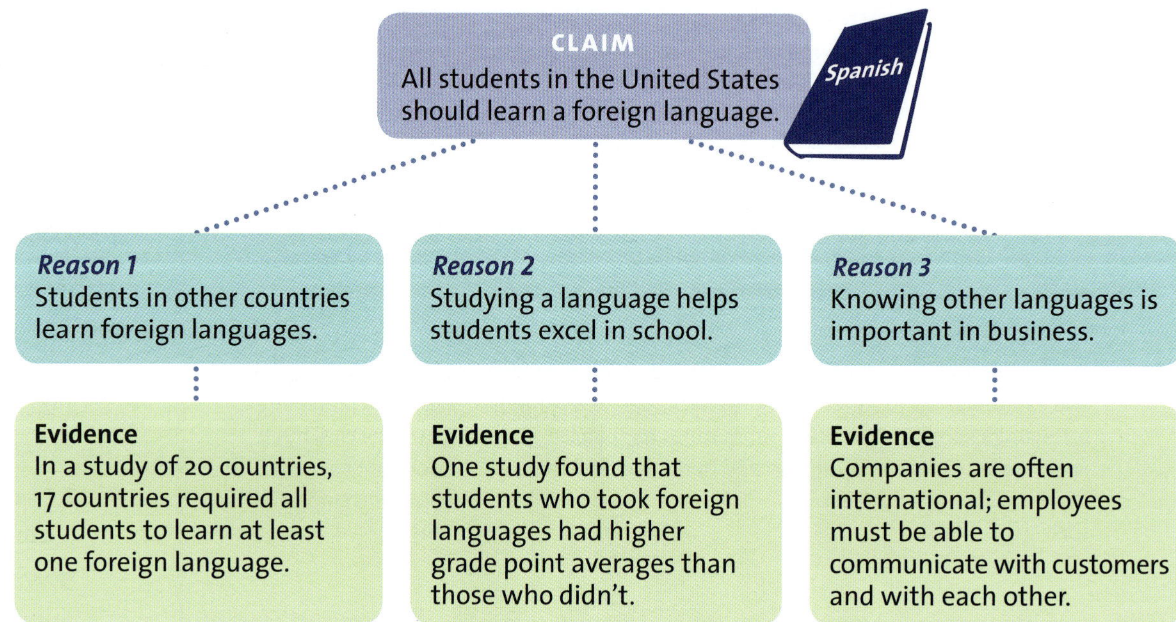

A **policy speech** is a speech that recommends a plan of action or a set of guidelines or rules to address an issue. It often contains the same elements as a written argument. In the following excerpt from a policy speech, Melinda Gates makes a claim about malaria, a disease that affects many children in Africa. As you read her speech, try to identify her claim. What is she urging her audience to do or believe? What reasons and evidence help her make her case?

from # Malaria Forum

Speech by **Melinda French Gates**

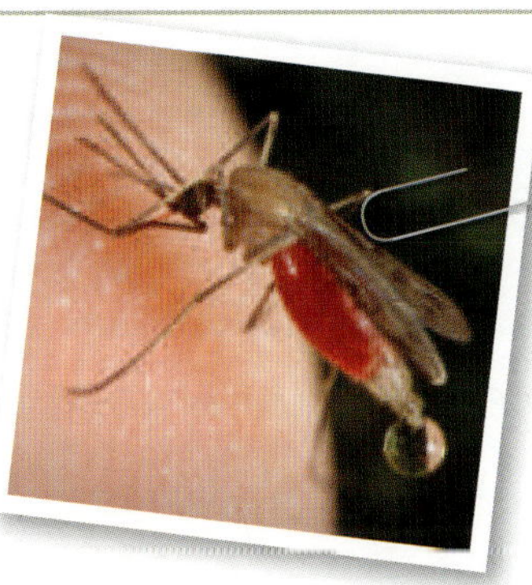

No child should die from malaria. No child. And the only way to end death from malaria is to end malaria.

It's fair to ask how is such a thing
5   possible? Is such a thing possible?

Here's how we see it. To eradicate malaria, you have to end transmission—and there are multiple points where you can intervene. Reduce the number of infected mosquitoes. Keep mosquitoes from biting people. Keep people who are bitten from getting infected. Keep
10   people who are infected from transmitting malaria back to mosquitoes.

Those are the intervention points. If we could find a tool that was one hundred percent effective, and if we could implement it completely at any one of these points, we would break the cycle of transmission and eradicate the disease.

15   This is just not possible today with the huge numbers of cases and the current tools. But it is possible—using the tools we have today, and addressing all the steps in a multi-pronged approach—to dramatically drive down the number of cases. Then, if we make the cases few enough, and the map of malaria small enough, we
20   could—theoretically—with a new vaccine, or a new medicine, or a new insecticide—identify and target one step in this cycle, totally stop transmission, and end the disease.

Close Read

1. Reread lines 1–7. What is Gates's claim about malaria?

2. In the boxed paragraph, Gates explains that one can interrupt the spread of malaria at multiple points. What evidence does she give to support this statement?

3. In the last paragraph, Gates explains why taking a multi-pronged approach would support her claim. In your own words, summarize this approach. Does she give evidence to support it?

Part 2: Persuasive Techniques and Rhetorical Fallacies

A writer will often use **persuasive techniques,** or methods intended to encourage you to accept his or her argument. Persuasive techniques use language to stir up people's emotions. The following appeals can be effective, but they are often used to disguise flaws in a weak argument.

Persuasive Technique	Definition	Example
Bandwagon Appeal	Suggests that a person should believe or do something because "everyone else" does it	"See the movie that everybody's talking about!"
Testimonial	Relies on endorsements from well-known people or satisfied customers	"As an Olympic athlete, I need a lot of energy. That's why I drink Quench-Ade."
Appeal to Pity, Fear, or Vanity	Uses strong feelings rather than facts to persuade	"Won't you give this abandoned puppy a home?"
Loaded Language	Uses words with strongly positive or negative connotations	"Start your day with Morning Glory's refreshing, all-natural juice."

In some cases, writers and speakers may use false or misleading statements known as **rhetorical fallacies** to persuade you to agree with them. Two examples of rhetorical fallacies are shown in the following chart.

Type of Fallacy	Definition	Example
Ad hominem	Attempts to discredit an idea by attacking the person's character rather than his or her argument	"My opponent cannot be trusted: Elect him, and city violence will surely increase."
Stereotyping	Makes a broad statement about people on the basis of their gender, ethnicity, race, or political, social, professional, or religious group	"All musicians think the same way."

MODEL 1: PERSUASION IN TEXT

The author of this editorial argues that playing video games can have some significant harmful effects. What techniques does the author use to persuade you to adopt his position?

from

Break the Addiction!

Editorial by **Ethan Flemming**

Hours disappear, and you don't notice. You spend all your money buying more. You think it's an effective way to relieve stress but you end up cutting yourself off from family, friends, and reality.

What started in living rooms across the country as a few hours here
5 and there has become an alarming widespread problem—a population addicted to video games. In fact, the average eighth-grade boy spends 23 hours a week playing video games, while the average eighth-grade girl spends 12 hours.

You may think that video games are just harmless fun, but studies
10 tell a more disturbing story. Some studies have concluded that excessive playing can decrease attention spans, dull imaginations, and create serious social problems. At least 60 percent of games are violent, and most teenagers cite those as their favorites. Repeatedly seeing violent situations unfold on a TV screen can take its toll. After all, such games
15 glamorize violent behavior and paint an unrealistic picture of the world.

Close Read

1. What emotion is the author appealing to in this editorial? Explain how the author might want readers to react to his message.

2. One example of loaded language is boxed. What bias might the author be revealing with this word? Find two more examples of loaded language.

MODEL 2: PERSUASION IN ADVERTISING

If you've turned on the television or skimmed a magazine recently, you know that persuasive techniques are used to sell all kinds of products, from soap to video games. What techniques do you notice in this ad?

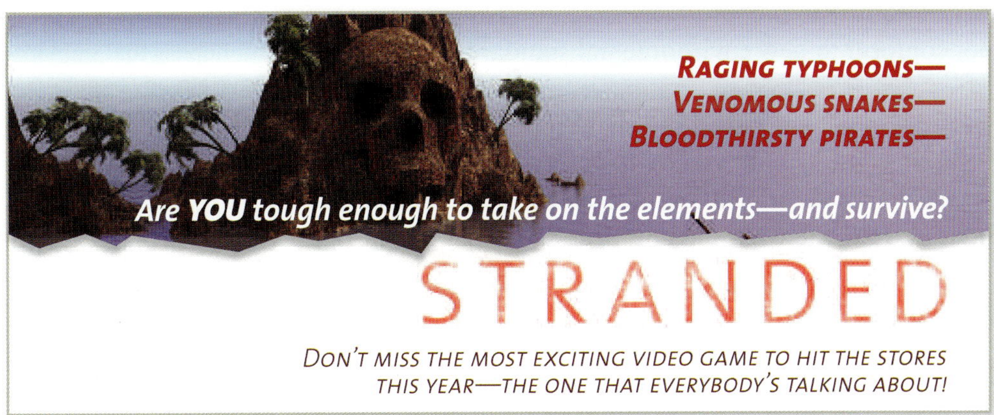

Close Read

1. Explain how this ad tries to appeal to your vanity.

2. Does this ad contain any rhetorical fallacies? Why or why not?

Part 3: Analyze the Text

In this essay, British scientist Jane Goodall shares her outlook on the future of the earth. Originally famous for studying the behaviors of chimpanzees in Africa, Goodall now travels around the world, speaking to people about the importance of protecting the environment. Read Goodall's essay, and then examine the public service ad that follows. What argument does each text present? What techniques does each use to persuade you?

THE PROMISE

Nonfiction article by **Jane Goodall**

As we begin the 21st century, it is easy to be overwhelmed by feelings of hopelessness. We humans have destroyed the balance of nature: forests are being destroyed, deserts are spreading, there is terrible pollution and poisoning of air, earth, water. Climate is changing, people are starving.
5   There are too many humans in some parts of the world, overconsumption in others. There is human cruelty to "man" and "beast" alike; there is violence and war. Yet I do have hope. Let me share my four reasons.

Firstly, we have at last begun to understand and face up to the problems that threaten the survival of the earth. And we are problem-
10 solving creatures. Our amazing brains have created modern technology, much of which has greatly benefited millions of people around the globe. Sadly, along with our tendency to overreproduce, it has also resulted in massive destruction and pollution of the natural world. But can we not use our awesome problem-solving ability to now find more
15 environmentally friendly ways to conduct our business? Good news—it's already happening as hundreds of industries and businesses adopt new "green" ethics.[1] And we must play our part—in our billions we must adopt less-harmful lifestyles. Refuse to buy products from companies, corporations, that do not conform to new environmental standards. We
20 *can* change the world.

Second, nature is amazingly resilient.[2] Given the chance, poisoned rivers can live again. Deforested land can be coaxed—or left—to blossom again. Animal species, on the verge of extinction, can sometimes be bred and saved from a few individuals.

---

1. **"green" ethics:** rules and guidelines that require businesses to use resources, machines, and procedures that are not harmful to the environment.

2. **resilient:** flexible.

25   My third reason for hope lies in the tremendous energy, enthusiasm, and commitment of young people around the world. Young people want to fight to right the wrongs, for it will be their world tomorrow—they will be the ones in leadership positions, and they themselves will be parents. . . .

    My fourth reason for hope lies in the indomitable[3] nature of the
30 human spirit. There are so many people who have dreamed seemingly unattainable dreams and, because they never gave up, achieved their goals against all the odds, or blazed a path along which others could follow.

    So let us move into the next millennium with hope—with faith in
35 ourselves, in our intelligence, in our indomitable spirit. Let us develop respect for all living things. Let us try to replace violence and intolerance with understanding and compassion and love.

---

3. **indomitable:** incapable of being defeated; unconquerable.

ACKNOWLEDGMENTS

Don Congdon Associates: "Dark They Were, and Golden-Eyed" as "The Naming of Names," from *Thrilling Wonder Stories* by Ray Bradbury. Copyright © 1949 by Standard Magazines, renewed 1976 by Ray Bradbury. Reprinted by permission of Don Congdon Associates, Inc.